W9-AVC-663

Ecosystems

Grasslands

Greg Reid

CHELSEA CLUBHOUSE

An Imprint of Chelsea House Publishers
A Haights Cross Communications Company

To Mary-Anne, Julian and Damian

This edition first published in 2004 in the United States of America by Chelsea Clubhouse, a division of Chelsea House Publishers and a subsidiary of Haights Cross Communications.

Chelsea Clubhouse
1974 Sproul Road, Suite 400
Broomall, PA 19008-0914

The Chelsea House world wide web address is www.chelseahouse.com

Library of Congress Cataloging-in-Publication Data Applied for.

ISBN 0-7910-7939-2

First published in 2004 by
MACMILLAN EDUCATION AUSTRALIA PTY LTD
627 Chapel Street, South Yarra, Australia, 3141

Associated companies and representatives throughout the world.

Copyright © Greg Reid 2004

Copyright in photographs © individual photographers as credited

Edited by Anna Fern and Miriana Dasovic
Text and cover design by Polar Design
Illustrations and maps by Alan Laver, Shelly Communications
Photo research by Legend Images

Printed in China

Acknowledgments

The author and publisher are grateful to the following for permission to reproduce copyright material:

Cover photograph: elephants in a tropical grassland, courtesy of Corbis Digital Stock.

Martin Harvey/ANTphoto.com.au, p. 25 (top); Jean-Paul Ferrero/Auscape International, p. 28; Ferrero-Labat/Auscape International, p. 20; Victoria Hurst/Auscape International, p. 13 (top right); Colin Monteath/Auscape International, pp. 5, 20; Australian Picture Library/Corbis, pp. 21, 27; Corbis Digital Stock, pp. 3 (center), 7, 11, 12 (main), 13 (top center), 15, 17 (both), 18 (top right), 25 (bottom), 29, 30 (left), 32; Legend Images, p. 12 (top); Hans & Judy Beste/Lochman Transparencies, p. 19; Dennis Sarson/Lochman Transparencies, p. 16; Pelusey Photography, pp. 6, 8; Photodisc, pp. 3 (top & bottom), 10, 13 (bottom), 14, 18 (top left & center), 18 (bottom left & right), 30 (right), 31; Photolibrary.com/SPL, p. 13 (top left); Stockbyte, p. 23; The G.R. "Dick" Roberts Photo Library, pp. 9, 22, 24, 26.

While every care has been taken to trace and acknowledge copyright, the publisher tenders their apologies for any accidental infringement where copyright has proved untraceable. Where the attempt has been unsuccessful, the publisher welcomes information that would redress the situation.

Please note

The author would like to thank Anatta Abrahams, Janine Hanna, Eulalie O'Keefe, Kerry Regan, Marcia Reid.

Contents

When a word is printed in **bold**, you can look up
its meaning in the Glossary on page 31.

What Are Grasslands?

Grasslands are places with vast, open plains of grass and fertile (rich) soils. A grassland environment is part of an ecosystem. An ecosystem is made up of living plants and animals and their non-living environment of air, water, energy, and nutrients.

Grasslands occupy about a quarter of the world's land surface. They are home to many unique plants, insects, **mammals**, birds, reptiles, and other animals. Some grasslands have huge herds of grazing animals, such as antelope, zebra, cattle, and sheep.

Low rainfall, **droughts**, and frequent fires stop large areas of trees from growing in grasslands. Because they have fertile soils, many grasslands have been cleared to grow important **cereal crops**, such as wheat and maize. These cleared areas are known as the world's "breadbaskets," because they supply food for the world.

Most grasslands are found between deserts and forests.

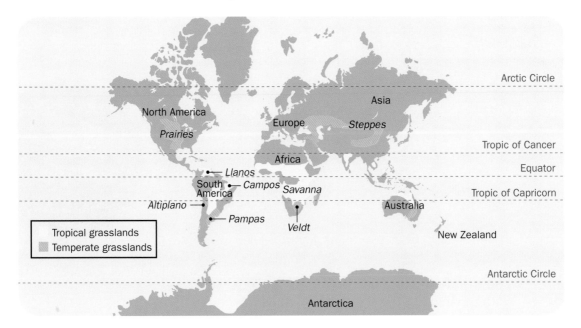

Where Do Grasslands Grow?

Grasslands cover almost half of the ice-free land on Earth. They grow on every continent except Antarctica. Grasslands form large areas between the dry deserts and the wet forests. Grasslands have different names in different parts of the world.

Some grasslands in the Southern Hemisphere lie on or near the east coast of continents.

Large grasslands are found behind mountains in the center of continents. This is because when clouds are forced to rise above mountains, they drop most of their rain on the mountains. Very little rain falls on the other side. The dry area behind mountains is called a rainshadow. These areas do not usually have many trees.

High Grasslands

The altiplano (high plain) in Bolivia, South America, is a grassy plain behind the Andes Mountains. It is so high that it is too cold for trees to grow. In summer, people move their herds of llamas there to graze on the grasses. In winter, the altiplano is covered in snow.

Horses grazing on the steppe of western Mongolia

Names of grasslands around the world

Continent	Grassland	Meaning of Name	Countries
Africa	Savanna Veldt	Tropical grassland Field	Kenya, Tanzania South Africa
Asia	Steppe	Grass plains	Russia, China, Mongolia
Australia	Downs	Grass plains	Australia
Europe	Puszta Steppe	Grass plains Grass plains	Hungary Russia, Ukraine
North America	Prairie	Grass plains	Canada, United States
South America	Altiplano Campos Llanos Pampas	High plain Field Plain Plain	Bolivia Brazil, Paraguay Venezuela Argentina, Uruguay

Types of Grasslands

There are two main types of grasslands, each with different climates, plants, and animals.

Temperate grasslands are found in cool temperate climates, often in the centers of continents such as Asia, North America, and the southern parts of Africa and South America. They are also found on or near the east coasts of continents, such as Australia and South America. Temperate grasslands lie outside the Tropic of Cancer and the Tropic of Capricorn. Here, grasses are the main plants.

Tropical grasslands, or savannas, are found in hot tropical climates. They lie between the Tropic of Cancer and the Tropic of Capricorn. Large areas of tropical grasslands are found in Africa, Australia, India, and South America. Here, grasses grow with shrubs and trees.

Campos tropical grassland in Brazil

Ecofact

Types of Grass

There are more than 11,000 species of grass in the world. Annual grasses grow for only part of the year, while perennial grasses grow all year. Grasses vary in size, from a few inches to several feet (a few centimeters to several meters) in height.

Short grasslands are used for grazing animals.

Tall and Short Grasslands

Grasslands are sometimes described using the height of the grasses. Grasslands can be tall, medium, or short. The height of the grasses depends on the rainfall they receive.

In wet areas near forests, grasslands have tall grass. Here, grasses such as African elephant grass may be more than 6.5 feet (2 meters) high. The soil in tall grassland areas usually has a thick layer of dark **humus** from the **decomposing** grasses over thousands of years. Because they grow in rich soils, most tall grasslands have been cleared for crops.

In dry areas near deserts, the grasses are much shorter. Short grassland soil only has a thin layer of humus because there is less decomposing grass. Many short grasslands are used for grazing animals such as cattle, sheep, and goats.

Temperate Grasslands

Temperate grasslands are found outside the tropics, usually behind mountains in the centers of continents. The large prairies of North America and the steppes of Europe and Asia have many other types of non-woody plants such as annuals, perennials, bulbs, and shrubs. Northern Hemisphere grasslands do not join up with any tropical grasslands.

Temperate grasslands of South America, Africa, and Australia are different from the Northern Hemisphere grasslands. The main types of plants in the pampas of South America are the tall feather grasses, such as pampas grass. Temperate grasslands in Australia and Africa join up with tropical grasslands. These adjoining grasslands share many of the same species of plants and animals. Temperate grasslands have a variety of plants and animals.

A temperate grassland in Chile

Temperate grasslands turn yellow in summer.

Climate

The climate of temperate grasslands varies with their location. Temperate grasslands close to the tropics have mild winters and hot summers. Farther away from the tropics, winter temperatures are cold and there can be strong winds. Snow and ice sometimes cover the grass. Summers are usually warm.

Rainfall in temperate grasslands varies as well. Near the desert areas, temperate grasslands with short grass get about 10 inches (250 millimeters) of rain a year. Near the forests, temperate grasslands with tall grass get about 30 inches (750 millimeters) of rain a year. Most rain falls in spring and early summer. The grass turns yellow in late summer as the soil dries out. Temperate grasslands have a variety of climates, and the plants and animals have adapted to this.

Temperate Grassland Plants

Temperate grassland plants and animals have many **adaptations** to help them survive. Temperate grasses have deep roots that can resist drought. Annual grasses grow quickly in dry areas after rain. They produce lots of seeds before they die. The annual grass seeds lie in the soil or are blown to other areas. Animals eat some seeds, but enough survive to grow into new plants when the rains arrive.

Perennial grasses have underground stems. New plants can grow from these stems as well as from grass seeds. Temperate grassland soil is thick with roots. The roots help to hold water in the soil and stop the soil from being washed or blown away.

A North American bison grazing in a wet prairie

Ecofact

Buffalo Grass

Buffalo grass and blue grama are short grasses found in the dry prairie of North America, near the Rocky Mountains. They grow only half an inch (about 1 centimeter) high and are good food for grazing animals, such as bison.

Temperate Grassland Animals

There are many species of temperate grassland insects, spiders, reptiles, birds, and mammals. Many birds nest on the ground because there are few trees. They have to be well **camouflaged**. Large herd animals, such as wildebeest and zebra, find safety in numbers as they move about looking for grass and water.

Types of animal adaptations in temperate grasslands

Animal Adaptation	Example of Animal
fast runners	saigas, guanacos, pronghorn, bisons, pampas deer, zebras, wolves, cheetahs, lions, coyotes, pumas
high jumpers	European hares, African springhaases, springboks, impalas, kangaroos
burrowers	prairie dogs, vischachas, sousliks, meerkats, **rodents** (mice, rats)
burrow hunters	ferrets, polecats, pampas cats, snakes
sky birds	skylarks, eagles, hawks, falcons
ground birds	ostriches, emus, rheas, grouses, burrowing owls

Ecofact

Bouncing Marsupials

Australian kangaroos and wallabies are well adapted to grasslands. These **marsupials** store fat in their tails and can go for days without a drink of water. Their bouncing movement also uses energy very efficiently.

The female kangaroo can carry its baby in its pouch as it hops along.

Large Herbivores

The largest animals in temperate grasslands are herbivores that live in herds and **migrate** in search of grass and water. These include the elephant, buffalo, zebra, and wildebeest from Africa, saiga, wild horses, and asses from Asia, kangaroos and wallabies from Australia, bison and pronghorn antelope from North America, and pampas deer from South America.

Some herds, such as the wildebeest herds of Africa, have hundreds of thousands of animals and migrate large distances from country to country following the seasonal rains. Herds in some areas have been reduced in numbers because people have taken the grasslands for farming and grazing their animals. As a result, the numbers of **predators**, such as lions and cheetahs, that hunt these herds have also fallen.

A large herd of wildebeest, migrating across grasslands in Africa

Ecofact

Fastest Land Bird

The African ostrich is the fastest bird that cannot fly. It can run at speeds of 45 miles (72 kilometers) an hour. Its stride may be more than 23 feet (7 meters) long.

African ostrich

Temperate Grassland Food Chains

Food chains show the feeding relationship between plants and animals. A food chain starts with the sun, water, and nutrients from the soil and decomposing plant and animal matter. These basic elements supply energy for plants. The next link in the chain occurs when herbivores and omnivores eat the plants. Herbivores eat only plants, while omnivores eat plants and other animals.

A food chain might continue with carnivores. These animals only eat meat. Carnivores are at the top of the food chain. When any plant or animal in the chain dies, worms and bacteria begin to decompose or break down the matter. The decomposed material returns to the soil, where plants take up the nutrients to grow, and the cycle continues.

Plant (North American blue stem grass) gets its energy from the Sun and nutrients from decaying matter and the soil.

1 →

2 Prairie dog (herbivore) eats blue stem grass.

Temperate grassland food chain in North America

3 Coyote (carnivore) eats prairie dog.

6 Blue stem grass takes up soil nutrients.

5 Golden eagle dies and is broken down by fungi and bacteria (decomposers).

4 ← Golden eagle (carnivore) eats coyote.

Tropical Grasslands

Tropical grasslands lie between the Tropic of Cancer and the Tropic of Capricorn. Africa, India, Australia, and South America have large areas of tropical grasslands. The largest area of tropical grasslands is in Africa, with about 40 percent of the continent being covered. Tropical grasslands in Africa are called savanna. This name is also used to describe tropical grasslands around the world.

Tropical grasslands in South America lie on either side of the rain forests of the Amazon Basin. In the north of the continent, tropical grasslands are called llanos. In the south, they are called campos.

In Australia and India, the tropical grasslands are mainly found inland. They are used for farming and grazing animals, such as cattle. Tropical grasslands have a wide range of plants and animals.

Ecofact

Large Herds of Herbivores

The savanna of Africa has more large-hoofed herbivores, such as wildebeests, antelopes, and zebras, than any other place on Earth. Millions of animals and many different species live there.

A large herd of springboks in the Kalahari Gemsbok National Park, South Africa

14

A tropical grassland in Africa during the wet season

Climate

Areas with tropical grasslands are warm all year. Tropical grasslands have a long dry season with drought, usually in winter. During this time, the grasses dry out and turn brown. Many waterholes and rivers dry up, and fires are common.

Tropical grasslands get most of their rain in summer. Sometimes, there are large thunderstorms. After rain, the grasses grow quickly and the grasslands turn green. Waterholes and rivers fill up, and animals breed because there is plenty of food and water. Tropical grasslands near forests may get more than 40 inches (1000 millimeters) of rain a year. Less rain falls in grassland areas near deserts.

Tropical grasslands have extremes of rainfall and drought, and the plants and animals have adapted to this.

Water-Bottle Trees

The baobab tree, from the tropical grasslands in Africa and Australia, has a swollen trunk that stores water. It is up to 33 feet (10 meters) in diameter. Baobabs are fire resistant and people and animals often use them for water. The baobab is also known as the "upside-down tree."

A baobab tree in Western Australia

Tropical Grassland Plants

There are many species of tropical grassland insects, spiders, reptiles, birds, and mammals. Tropical grassland plants and animals have many adaptations to help them survive.

Different combinations of grass and trees in tropical grasslands produce four main types of **habitat**. Close to deserts, there is grassland savanna with very few trees. Parkland savanna is where trees cover 10 percent of the area. Thick savanna has from 10 to 50 percent of the area covered by trees. Savanna woodland is in the wettest areas, where trees cover 50 to 90 percent of the area.

Grasses are up to 12 feet (4 meters) tall in the wetter areas, and only 3 feet (1 meter) in the drier areas. Grasses in tropical grasslands are taller than temperate grasslands because the climate is warmer throughout the year.

Tropical grassland plants have adapted to seasonal drought. Some trees, such as acacias, have small, thorny leaves to reduce water loss. Eucalyptus trees in Australia have leathery leaves for the same reason.

Tropical Grassland Animals

There are many different habitats in tropical grasslands, so there is a wide variety of animal species too. The savannas of eastern Africa have more grassland animals than any other ecosystem. There are about 40 species of antelope, such as gazelle, impala, kudu, and springbok. Each species has adapted to feed in a special way so it does not compete with other antelope species. Some species eat short grass, while others eat long grass or tree leaves.

There are also many different types of carnivores in African tropical grasslands. These predators have many adaptations to help them survive. Some carnivores, such as lions, hunting dogs, and hyenas, hunt in groups for better hunting success. Leopards, genets, and civets are well camouflaged for life in the trees.

An African spotted hyena, yawning

Cheetahs: the Fastest Land Animal

The cheetah lives in the tropical grasslands of Africa and Asia. This cat is the fastest land animal. It can reach speeds of 70 miles (112 kilometers) an hour for short distances while chasing its **prey**.

A cheetah speeds after its prey.

Tropical Grassland Food Chains

Tropical grassland plants and animals are connected in food chains. Here is an example of a food chain from a tropical grassland in Africa. **Scavengers**, such as vultures, usually eat any dead animals and the remains of kills by other animals.

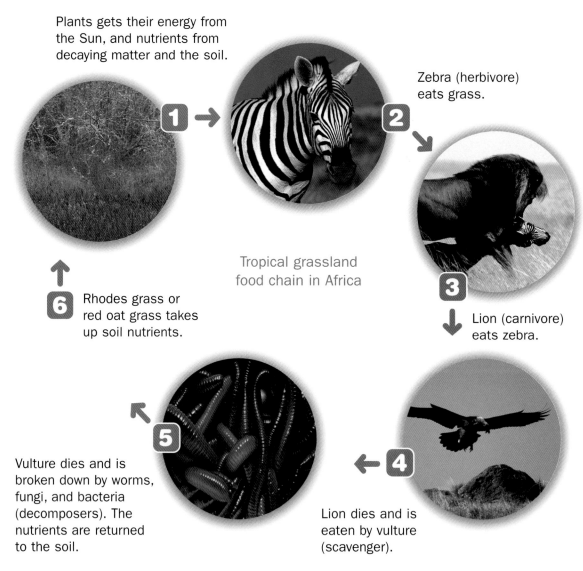

Plants gets their energy from the Sun, and nutrients from decaying matter and the soil.

Zebra (herbivore) eats grass.

Tropical grassland food chain in Africa

Rhodes grass or red oat grass takes up soil nutrients.

Lion (carnivore) eats zebra.

Vulture dies and is broken down by worms, fungi, and bacteria (decomposers). The nutrients are returned to the soil.

Lion dies and is eaten by vulture (scavenger).

Animal Relationships

In Africa, oxpecker birds (or tickbirds) eat the **parasitic ticks** that live on the skin of large herbivores, such as antelope and rhinoceros. Both animals benefit from this. The birds get a reliable source of food, and the large herbivores get rid of their pests. Oxpeckers also make a hissing sound to warn the large animals when predators are near.

Egrets follow large animals, such as buffalos and rhinoceroses, and eat grasshoppers and other insects that are disturbed by the grazing animals.

Zebras and wildebeest are often found together in large herds in Africa. They feed on different levels of grasses and do not compete with each other for food. The animals benefit from being together by being able to spot predators more quickly.

Giraffes in Kenya, Africa, eating from the treetops

Indigenous Peoples

Indigenous peoples have lived in grasslands for thousands of years. Aboriginal peoples from Australia, the Hadza from Africa, and the Native American Indians such as the Apache once hunted animals and gathered food in grasslands. Today, very few people live like this because many grasslands are now used for farming and grazing animals, such as cattle and sheep.

Indigenous peoples in some grasslands graze herds of animals. On the Asian steppes, **nomads**, such as the Khalkha Mongols, live off the milk and meat from their herds of sheep, goats, yaks, camels, and horses. In eastern Africa, the Masai move their herds of cattle around dry savanna grasslands. The way of life of nomadic people is under threat, as more grasslands are taken up for farming and grazing.

Masai men herding cattle in Kenya, Africa

Ecofact

Mobile Homes

The nomads of the Asian steppes live in tents made from animal skins and wool, called yurts. Yurts can be easily packed up and carried when the animals are moved to new areas.

Yurts in western Mongolia

Grassland Farmers

In the wetter areas of the African savannas, people live in villages and small towns. They grow crops and raise animals on small areas of land. The men usually clear the land, and the women plant and look after the crops.

The types of crops grown depend on how much water there is. Millet is grown in dry areas, while maize is grown in wet areas. Some crops are **irrigated** from wells or rivers. Crops include yams, wheat, cassava, cotton, sorghum, and vegetables. Crops sometimes fail because of droughts, and the people starve. Savanna farmers usually depend on the wet season to provide water for their crops, and grass for their animals.

Plowing the soil to grow crops on a grassland in Zimbabwe, Africa

Grassland Resources

The most valuable resource of many grasslands is their flat land with rich soil and few trees. These conditions are ideal for farming and grazing. This is why many grasslands have been cleared.

Some **domesticated** plants and animals originated in grasslands. Cereals such as wheat, oats, barley, rice, sorghum, and rye originally came from the steppes of Europe and Asia. Maize originally came from North and Central America. Horses, cattle, ostriches, sheep, and goats originated in Asia, Europe, and Africa.

Cereals were once wild grasses. People first started to grow wild einkorn, emmer wheat, and wild barleys about 10,000 years ago around the Middle East. Today, many grassland areas are used for growing cereal crops and grazing livestock. Grasslands have provided many valuable resources for people.

Ecofact

Valuable Grasslands

Most of the world's cereals and meat come from grasslands. These are worth about $250 billion a year to farmers around the world.

Cereal crops on the Canadian prairie

Food for the World

Grassland areas produce most of the world's food. About 42 percent of grasslands are used for grazing animals, and about 20 percent are used for growing cereal crops. Cereals are the most important crops grown in the world. They are made into bread, cookies, porridge, and pasta. Cereals are also fed to domestic animals such as pigs, cattle, horses, and poultry.

Wheat, oats, maize, and rye grow best in temperate grassland areas, while barley and sorghum grow best in tropical grassland areas. Sheep are usually grazed in temperate grassland areas. Some types of cattle, such as Herefords, prefer temperate grassland areas. Other types of cattle, such as Zebu, prefer tropical grassland areas because they can survive hot, dry conditions. Some of the most productive farmland in the world was once grassland.

A field of wheat

Ecofact

Food Belts

Farmers in some grassland areas grow one main cereal crop. These areas are sometimes named after the cereal. The prairies of the United States have a "corn belt," and Australia has a "wheat belt."

Threats to Grasslands

The biggest threat to grasslands is clearing. When grasslands are cleared, the plants and animals are threatened. Food chains are broken, and many plants and animals become extinct in that area. About 98 percent of the tall grass prairie of the United States has been cleared for farming and the building of roads, railways, and towns.

Another threat to grasslands is overgrazing by domestic animals. This can kill native plants and leave the soil bare and open to **erosion** by wind and water. In dry grassland areas and in droughts, this can lead to **dust bowls**.

In some grasslands, imported grasses and weeds can take over from the native grasses. Herbicides used to control weeds sometimes kill native grasses. Grasslands are an endangered ecosystem that is under threat from many sources.

Ecofact

Chemical Sprays

Chemicals used to control insects and weeds on modern farms also harm grassland plants and animals. When insects die, other links in the food chain, such as birds and small animals, suffer.

Overgrazed country in Australia

Threatened Plants and Animals

Today, many grassland plants and animals are endangered because their habitat is being lost. Two Australian grassland plants have become extinct in the past 200 years, and 19 species of grass are endangered. Many grasses survive only in special parks or places such as roadsides, railway sidings, and old cemeteries.

Poaching endangers some animals, such as rhinoceroses, which are hunted for their horn. The bison of the North American prairie was almost extinct because of over-hunting. In 1892, there were only 85 bison left from a population of 60 to 125 million animals. Today, there are more than 150,000 bison living in special reserves and private ranches. More grassland areas need to be protected so the threatened plants and animals can survive.

Bison grazing in Yellowstone National Park, Wyoming, United States

Ecofact

Wild Dogs

African wild dogs live in packs in savannas. They are Africa's most successful hunters, but they are being threatened by farmers shooting them, and diseases carried by domestic dogs.

Effects of Clearing Grasslands

When grasslands are cleared, the links in food chains are disturbed. Farmland does not provide good habitat for large grassland herbivores and carnivores, and they die out or move away. Even small grassland animals, such as prairie dogs and meercats, find it hard to survive in the changed ecosystem. Fires, which are a natural event in grasslands, are controlled so they do not damage farmland.

Once grassland soil is plowed, the root system of the grasses is destroyed. The soil may then be blown or washed away. In some grassland areas, excess salts have been left behind by crop irrigation water. Too much salt in the soil kills the plants. Grassland soils need to be looked after because they are easily damaged.

An eroded gully in a cleared grassland area

Desertification

In some developing countries in Africa and Asia, grasslands on the edge of deserts are under pressure from poor farming practices, growing populations, and regular droughts. Some grassland areas have turned into desert. This is called desertification.

Grazing too many animals, such as goats and cattle, can kill grassland plants. When farmers clear grasslands and plow the soil, wind can easily blow the soil away. In times of drought, the crops fail, animals die, and people suffer. As a result, the deserts grow larger. Grassland areas need to be managed to stop the spread of deserts.

This area in southern Africa was once covered in grass, but is now barren due to drought and overgrazing.

Ecofact

Goats: Four-Legged Locusts

Goats are popular animals in African grasslands. They eat any plants and are easy to look after. However, too many goats in an area can eat all the plants and turn grasslands into deserts.

Protecting Grasslands

Small areas of original grassland still exist in some farmland areas. Governments and conservation groups are working to protect some of these rare areas.

Some larger grassland areas are also being protected in national parks and reserves. Here, the endangered plants and animals have a greater chance of survival. In Africa, some large parks run across different countries. These are called **transfrontier parks**. Mozambique, Zimbabwe, and South Africa plan to set up the Great Limpopo Transfrontier Park, which would combine three savanna parks in the three countries. Savanna parks are very popular with ecotourists because they contain much wildlife. More needs to be done to protect what few grassland ecosystems remain, before it is too late.

Big Blue Stem Grass

In the 1980s, only 3.9 square miles (10 square kilometers) out of about 38,610 square miles (100,000 square kilometers) of big blue stem grass was left in Illinois. The University of Illinois set up a reserve of 11.7 square miles (30 square kilometers) in which to grow the endangered plant.

Kruger National Park, in South Africa, will be part of Great Limpopo Transfrontier Park.

Ecotourism in Grasslands

Ecotourism is when visitors pay to see the beauty of a natural ecosystem. People want to see wildlife in a natural grassland habitat. Ecotourism does not cause much disturbance to the grasslands. In many areas, governments and local people can earn more money from tourists visiting grasslands than from clearing the grasslands.

Some special grassland areas, such as Masai Mara National Park in Kenya and Yellowstone National Park in the United States, are protected. Wildlife tours to savanna parks are very popular in many African countries, such as South Africa and Tanzania. Indigenous people can become guides for visitors. Ecotourism can help protect grassland plants and animals for the future.

Ecofact

Lion's Share

A single lion in a savanna park in Kenya is worth $US270,000 a year from ecotourism. Fifty times more money is made from ecotourism in Kenya than from farming.

Ecotourists observing wildlife in a natural habitat help protect ecosystems.

How to Save Grasslands

We can all work to save grasslands. Learn more about the importance of grasslands to the world. Join a conservation group and let others know about the threats to grasslands and the threats of deserts growing larger. Write to the government and ask them to help save more habitats in grasslands. The governments of rich countries can help poor countries protect their grasslands for the good of everyone.

ecosystems

The following web sites give more information on grasslands.

Grassland
http://www.enchantedlearning.com/biomes/grassland/grassland.shtml

Grassland biomes
http://curriculum.calstatela.edu/courses/builders/lessons/less/biomes/grass/grassland.html

Grasslands
http://mbgnet.mobot.org/sets/grasslnd/index.htm

The grassland biome
http://oncampus.richmond.edu/academics/as/education/projects/webunits/biomes/grass.html

The world's biomes
http://www.ucmp.berkeley.edu/glossary/gloss5/biome/grasslan.html

Glossary

adaptations	changes that help plants and animals survive in an environment
camouflaged	describes an animal whose color or shape helps it to blend into the background
cereal crops	plants, such as wheat and rice, that were once wild grasses
decomposing	breaking down
domesticated	plants and animals that humans have grown or tamed
droughts	times of water shortage that cause stress to plants, animals, and people
dust bowls	areas of land which have been turned into desert and which are affected by wind erosion
erosion	the removal of soil and rocks by wind, water, or ice
habitat	the environment in which an organism lives
humus	rich, decaying plant material in the top layer of the soil
indigenous peoples	groups of people who first lived in a place, whose traditional ways help them to survive in that place
irrigated	when crops are watered by a system of pipes or channels
mammals	a group of animals that have hair or fur, warm blood, a large brain, and feed their young milk
marsupials	a group of mammals that carry their young in a pouch
migrate	to move from one area to another
nomads	people who move from place to place instead of living in one spot
parasitic ticks	small insects that feed off another animal
poaching	the hunting of animals that are protected
predators	animals that hunt and eat other animals
prey	animals that are hunted and eaten by predators
rodents	small mammals with sharp front teeth
scavengers	animals that live off dead animals
transfrontier parks	parks that spread across several countries

Index